RICHARD MacANDREW and CATHY LAWDAY

The Nigh

For further information on the full
levels in the series, please contact
catalogue

HEINEMANN ELT

Series Editor: John Milne

The Heinemann ELT Guided Readers provide a choice of enjoyable reading material for learners of English. The series is published at five levels – Starter, Beginner, Elementary, Intermediate and Upper. At **Beginner Level**, the control of content and language has the following main features:

Information Control

The stories are written in a fluent and pleasing style with straightforward plots and a restricted number of main characters. The cultural background is made explicit through both words and illustrations. Information which is vital to the story is clearly presented and repeated where necessary.

Structure Control

Special care is taken with sentence length. Most sentences contain only one clause, though compound sentences are used occasionally with the clauses joined by the conjunctions 'and', 'but', and 'or'. The use of these compound sentences gives the text balance and rhythm. The use of Past Simple and Past Continuous Tenses is permitted since these are the basic tenses used in narration and students must become familiar with these as they continue to extend and develop their reading ability.

Vocabulary Control

At **Beginner Level** there is a controlled vocabulary of approximately 600 basic words, so that students with a basic knowledge of English will be able to read with understanding and enjoyment. Help is also given in the form of vivid illustrations which are closely related to the text.

For further information on the full selection of Readers at all five levels in the series, please refer to the Heinemann ELT Readers catalogue.

1
The River

It was six o'clock in the morning and it was dark. Ten-year-old Mark Watson picked up his bag and left the house. He was going fishing.

He walked to the river and sat down.

After more than an hour he had some luck. There was a fish on his line. Quickly he pulled in the line. It was a big fish – he was very happy.

The fish was a strange colour and it smelt strange, too. He didn't know what kind of fish it was. But he put it in his bag and went home.

Mark arrived home. He went into the kitchen. His father was making breakfast.

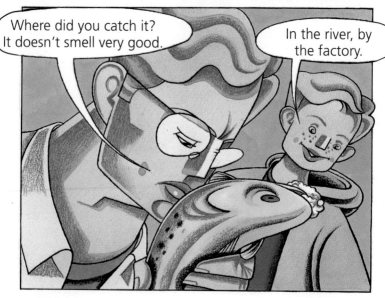

THE COURIER

DANGER FROM RIVER POLLUTION

by Emma Patel

Ten years ago, the River Oster was clean and beautiful. Today it is very polluted. It is dirty and dangerous!

People in Osterfield have to be careful. I talked to Dr Platt at the West Osterfield Hospital. 'Last month a nine-year-old boy, Kevin Walker, fell into the river. He swallowed a lot of river water and he almost died! Pollution has made the water very dangerous,' said Dr Platt. 'Do not drink the water – it is full of poisons. And do not eat fish from the river – you will become very ill,' Dr Platt told me.

Where do these poisons come from? From the factories along the river. Every month, more and more poisons go into the river.

The Courier asks: When is this pollution going to stop? Our reporter tried to talk to the owner of one of the factories, Milford's Chemicals. But he was 'too busy'.

2

Professor Hamilton's Laboratory

It was 5.30 on Friday evening. Three people were in their laboratory at Oster Valley University. Professor Hamilton, Dr Andrew Scott and Jo, the laboratory assistant, were working together.

'I have to go now,' said Professor Hamilton. 'I'm flying to Zurich very early tomorrow morning and I need some sleep.'

Andrew looked up from his work.

'Will you be back on Monday?' he asked.

'No, I'm coming back on Tuesday. I'm going to a meeting on Monday morning. Then I'm going to spend the afternoon with Professor Fischer. He's going to show me his new laboratory in Zurich. I'm flying back on Monday night. I'll see you both on Tuesday morning.'

'Have a good journey, Professor,' said Andrew.

'I hope you both have a good rest this weekend. And don't worry about work,' said Professor Hamilton. She put on her coat.

'OK,' said Jo. 'And don't talk to Professor Fischer about our work!'

They all laughed.

'Don't worry! I won't!' said the professor. 'I'm going now. See you on Tuesday.'

The professor left. Then Jo left a few minutes later. At about 6.30, Andrew finished work. He turned off the lights and locked the laboratory door.

8

Andrew walked through the university gardens to the bus stop. A dark-haired young woman was waiting at the bus stop. Her name was Faridah. She worked in another laboratory at the university and Andrew knew her well.

'Hi, Andrew! I haven't seen you for a long time. How are you?'

'I'm fine, thanks, Faridah. How about you? Is your laboratory busy at the moment?'

'Oh, not very busy! What's happening in your lab? Are you still studying pollution?'

'Yes. We're studying the problem of river pollution.'

'I read the report about river pollution in the newspaper,' said Faridah.

'Yes. The pollution is terrible,' Andrew replied. 'Plants and fish are dying. A boy almost died last month.'

'Isn't the government trying to stop pollution?'

'Yes. But they can't check all the factories all the time. Sometimes the police find out that a factory is polluting a river. The factory pays a fine – but it is never very much money.'

'The owners of the factories don't worry about the pollution. They want to make money!' said Faridah.

'That's right,' said Andrew. 'We're trying to make a new chemical compound. We want a compound to clean the water in the river. We want to stop the poisons killing the plants and fish.

'But the factories won't spend a lot of money to stop their pollution. We have to make a cheap compound – and that's difficult.'

'Aren't other universities studying river pollution too?' asked Faridah.

'Yes. Professor Fischer, at the University of Zurich, is also trying to make a new chemical compound.'

'Oh no! That's bad news!'

'Yes, it is. We want to make the compound first! We want to be famous!' replied Andrew. He laughed.

11

'We think our work is almost finished,' Andrew went on. 'But we think Professor Fischer is doing well, too!'

'So perhaps he will find the compound first?' asked Faridah.

'Yes. Unfortunately he has a better laboratory. Professor Hamilton is going to Zurich this weekend. She's going to see his new lab.'

'He won't give her any help!' said Faridah.

'No!' said Andrew. 'Professor Fischer isn't going to tell her anything!'

'And Professor Hamilton isn't going to tell him anything about your work! Look … here's my bus. Bye, Andrew.'

'Bye Faridah. Have a good weekend!'

3

Working Late

When he arrived home, Andrew cooked a meal. He ate a little, but he wasn't hungry. He turned on the television, but turned it off after a few minutes. He was thinking about work.

The telephone rang.

'Hi, Andrew. Barry here. Steve and I are going out for a Chinese meal. Do you want to come?'

'No, thanks, Barry. I'm tired ...'

'Come on, Andrew. It's Friday night! You don't have to work tomorrow.'

'No, I'm sorry. I'm very tired.'

'OK. Bye.'

'Bye, Barry.'

At about 10.30, Andrew left his flat and went for a walk.

'Professor Hamilton told me not to worry about work,' he thought. 'But she's going to be in Zurich. She's going to meet people, talk, work. She'll be busy. I have nothing to do this weekend. I want to work. I'm sure we can find the compound first.'

He walked round the town for a long time. Then he walked towards the university.

Andrew arrived at the laboratory at 11.30. He took out his keys and unlocked the door. Everything was dark and quiet. He got out his papers and read them.

'We haven't got much time,' he thought.

Andrew sat down and started work.

Suddenly the door opened and a light shone in his face. He couldn't see anything.

'What's happening?' he shouted.

'Who are you? What are you doing?' a voice asked him.

'Who are YOU?' Andrew asked.

'The police. What are you doing here?'

'I work here. I'm Dr Andrew Scott. Look, here's my university identity card. I work with Professor Hamilton. What's the matter?'

The young police officer took Andrew's university identity card and looked at it.

'OK, OK, don't worry. I'm sorry, Dr Scott. We were driving past the university and we saw a light. I came in to check that everything was all right.'

'Oh. I was working. What time is it?'

'Almost five a.m.'

'Is it? I've been here all night. I'm working hard on something important. I haven't looked at the clock.'

Then the door opened and another police officer came in.

'Is everything all right?'

'Yes, there's no problem,' replied the young police officer.

'Good. We have to go. I've had a radio message. There's been a bad accident on the road to the airport. Let's go.'

'I'm coming. Goodbye, Dr Scott. I'm sorry. I didn't mean to give you a shock.'

'That's all right.'

The two police officers left the lab. Andrew stood up and walked around. He was very tired and thirsty. He went and made a cup of coffee.

4

The Accident

The police car stopped near the ambulance. Lights shone through the thick fog.

Two people were standing at the edge of the road beside a van. A car was lying in a field, burning. The police officers got out of their car. An ambulanceman came towards them.

'What happened?' asked the young police officer.

'It's a bad accident. There was a crash in the fog. The red car went off the road and went into that field. The two people from the van are all right. But the driver of the red car is dead.'

'Was the car burning when you arrived?' asked the other police officer.

'No,' the ambulanceman replied. 'I pulled the driver out first. Then the fire started.'

'Do you know who the driver is?' asked the young police officer. 'Is there any identification?'

'No. The driver was a woman. But her bag burnt in the car. I couldn't get it.'

'Is there anything in her pockets?'

'I don't know,' said the ambulanceman. 'I didn't have time to look.'

'OK. I'll look now,' the young police officer said.

He went into the ambulance.

After a few minutes, he came out with a piece of paper in his hand.

'I've found this.'

The Travel Shop

14 Valley Road
Osterfield OS4 5DW
(0692) 473912

Here are your tickets.

You are flying
on: BA 5603

Your plane leaves Easton airport
at: 0700

on: Saturday, 16th October

You arrive in ZURICH

at: 0815

Please be at the airport at: 0530

Your Travel Check list

Have you got your:

passport ☐

money ☐

tickets ☐

Have you booked: a hotel ☐

a car ☐

Have a good journey!
Please book with us again!

5

Professor Hamilton Returns

In the laboratory, Andrew Scott was working hard. Suddenly he felt a cold wind and his papers fell on the floor. The door opened. Andrew looked up. There was Professor Hamilton! He was very surprised to see her.

'What are you doing here?' he asked.

'I'm going to help you,' she replied.

'But I don't understand … why aren't you in Zurich? Did you miss your plane? What about your meetings?'

'You ask too many questions! I had to come back. I had to finish the work.'

The professor sat down next to Andrew.

'Let's start. Now, show me what have you done.'

'I came back at midnight last night,' he said. 'I did some of the experiments again – here, look.'

Professor Hamilton looked at Andrew's papers.

'We can make this new compound, Andrew. I know we can,' she said. 'I've got an idea. Let's try something very different ...'

The two of them began to work together.

Andrew and the professor worked hard all Saturday morning. At about two o'clock Andrew was feeling hungry.

'Can we stop for a few minutes?' he asked. 'I'm very hungry. I haven't eaten since last night – and I didn't eat much then.'

'Of course,' said the professor. 'I'm sorry, Andrew. I didn't think. Go and get something to eat now. The university café is open on Saturdays.'

'Are you coming?'

'No. I'll stay here.'

'Aren't you hungry? Shall I bring you something to eat, Professor?'

'No, thanks. I'm all right.'

A little later, Andrew hurried back from the café.
The two scientists continued to work.

———

It became dark outside.

'It's late, Andrew. Go home – you're very tired.'

'Oh, no! I can't go home now – this is too exciting!
I've been here almost twenty-four hours. We've almost
finished now. I'm staying until the end.'

The professor laughed.

'OK. You're right. It is exciting. We're going to beat
Professor Fischer.'

At 3 a.m. Professor Hamilton sat back in her seat. She pointed at the computer screen. 'That's it, Andrew,' she said quietly, 'We've made the compound.'

'Yes, yes! Isn't it great?' Andrew shouted. 'We've done it! Who can we tell? Let's go and tell Jo! Let's have a party!'

'No, no,' said the professor. 'It's three o'clock in the morning. Wait until later. Go home now. You need some sleep, Andrew.'

'Yes, you're right. I'm very tired. I need a bath, a meal and some sleep.'

Professor Hamilton picked up their papers and locked them in a cupboard. Andrew put on his coat and went out of the laboratory. At the door, he looked round at the professor.

'Isn't it wonderful? We've made the compound and beaten Professor Fischer!'

'Yes,' she said. 'Go on, go home now.'

'OK. See you tomorrow.'

The professor smiled. She said nothing.

6

Strange News

Andrew walked home through the dark streets. He arrived at his flat at about four o'clock. Immediately he went to bed. He slept for more than twelve hours. When he woke up, he thought about the two nights at the laboratory. He thought about his work with Professor Hamilton. Was it all a dream?

He turned on the radio.

One person died early yesterday morning when two cars crashed in the fog. The accident happened on the A329 between Osterfield and Easton airport.

The accident! Andrew remembered now! Two police officers had come to the laboratory early on Saturday morning. They had gone to that accident. So it wasn't a dream. He had been at the lab. He had worked with Professor Hamilton. They had finished their work!

He got out of bed and went to the phone. He tried to phone Jo. He wanted to tell her the good news. But there was no reply. Perhaps she was away for the weekend. He tried to phone Professor Hamilton, too. But there was no reply.

Andrew made a meal and then he tried to phone the professor again. But again there was no reply.

He sat down and watched the television. Soon a film started. It was an old black and white film called 'A Visit from the Dead'. Andrew watched it and then went back to bed.

On Monday morning, Andrew arrived early at the university. He was very happy. He couldn't wait. He had to tell everybody the good news.

He went into the laboratory. Jo and the professor had not arrived. He got out his keys and unlocked the cupboard. He took out his papers. He read them again.

The door opened and Jo came in. Andrew jumped up from his chair.

'Have you heard? Have you heard?' he shouted.

'Yes,' replied Jo. She looked sad. 'It's terrible news. I'm very sorry.'

'Terrible news? Very sorry? What do you mean? It's wonderful news!'

'What are you talking about, Andrew?'

'Our work! Professor Hamilton and I have finished it. We worked together here all day on Saturday and all Saturday night. It's finished. We've done it!'

He held up the papers.

Jo looked at Andrew and said nothing.

'What's wrong?' asked Andrew. 'Aren't you happy about it? Professor Hamilton and I – we've made the compound! And we've made it before Professor Fischer!'

'I don't understand,' said Jo. 'Professor Hamilton is dead. She died in a car accident. She was driving to the airport and she had a crash in the fog. I tried to phone you on Saturday night. But there was no reply.'

'You're wrong,' said Andrew. 'Professor Hamilton and I were here. She was here with me.'

'No. She died at about five o'clock on Saturday morning. Look – it's all here, in the newspaper.'

7

Twenty Years Later

Twenty years later, Professor Andrew Scott was walking beside the River Oster.

A few metres away, Mark Watson and his young daughter were fishing.

'Look, Dad! I've caught something!' shouted the girl.

'Quick. Pull it in. Oh, that's a big fish!'

'Can we eat it, Dad? Can we take it home and cook it?'

'Of course we can.'

Andrew smiled. He looked at the river. The water was clean now.

He was thinking about Professor Hamilton and their work together twenty years ago.

'That was a very strange weekend,' he thought. 'Nobody believed my story about Professor Hamilton.'

People had told him, 'The professor is dead. She wasn't in the laboratory with you. You dreamt it. But we understand. You were very tired. You worked hard, with no sleep for over thirty hours. We understand. You did the work alone.'

Andrew stopped on a bridge and looked down at the river. The water was clean now. There was no more pollution. He watched the water below his feet. He thought about that night twenty years ago. Andrew remembered the cold wind when Professor Hamilton came through the door of the laboratory. Andrew remembered her quiet voice.

'We can make this new compound, Andrew. I know we can.'

'It was a dream,' said Andrew. 'I was tired. She didn't come back that night. She was dead. These things don't happen.'

Or do they?

Macmillan Heinemann English Language Teaching, Oxford

A division of Macmillan Publishers Limited

Companies and representatives throughout the world

ISBN 0 435 27183 0

Heinemann is a registered trade mark of Reed Educational and Professional Publishing Ltd

© Richard MacAndrew and Cathy Lawday 1995
First published 1995

This is a work of fiction. Any similarities to people,
institutions, corporations or public bodies bearing
the same name is purely coincidental.

Illustrated by Fiona MacVicar/The Inkshed
Typography by Adrian Hodgkins
Designed by Sue Vaudin
Cover by Jake Abrams and Threefold Design
Typeset in 12/16pt Goudy
Printed and bound in Malta by Interprint Limited

2003   2002   2001   2000   1999
  9   8   7   6   5